Kaori and the Lizard King

Robert Campbell & Piet Peterson

STARTER LEVEL

Material written by: Robert Campbell
Special thanks to Lindsay Clandfield

Commissioning Editor: Jacquie Bloese

Editor: Carolyn Barraclough

Cover design: Dawn Wilson

Designer: Dawn Wilson

Picture research: Emma Bree

Photo credits:
Page 26: Mary Glasgow Magazines.
Page 27: BVI/Everett/Rex Features; AMPAS/AFP/Getty Images. **Pages 28 & 29:** Disney/BVI; AFP/Getty Images; New Line, E. Wing/Rex Features.

Illustrations: Piet Peterson

No part of this publication may be reproduced in whole or in part, or stored in a retrieval system, or transmitted in any form or by any means, electronic, mechanical, photocopying, recording or otherwise, without written permission of the publisher. For information regarding permission write to:

Mary Glasgow Magazines (Scholastic Inc.)
Euston House
24 Eversholt Street
London
NW1 1DB

© Robert Campbell & Piet Luthi 2006
All rights reserved.

Printed in Singapore

Contents | Page

Kaori and the Lizard King | 4–25

People and places | **4**

Kaori and the Lizard King | **6–25**

Fact Files | 26–29

Manga facts | **26**

Fantasy worlds | **28**

Self-Study Activities | 29–32

New Words! | see inside back cover

PEOPLE AND PLACES

Kaori and the Lizard King

KAORI
Kaori is 13. She goes to Lucertola High School. She's in love with Jeff.

LUCERTOLA
Lucertola is a beautiful island. There are lots of beaches on the island and one mountain, Mount Oscurola.

There are lots of lizards on the island, but not many children.

Lucertola is very hot and it doesn't rain very often. There isn't much water. Why? Something is happening…

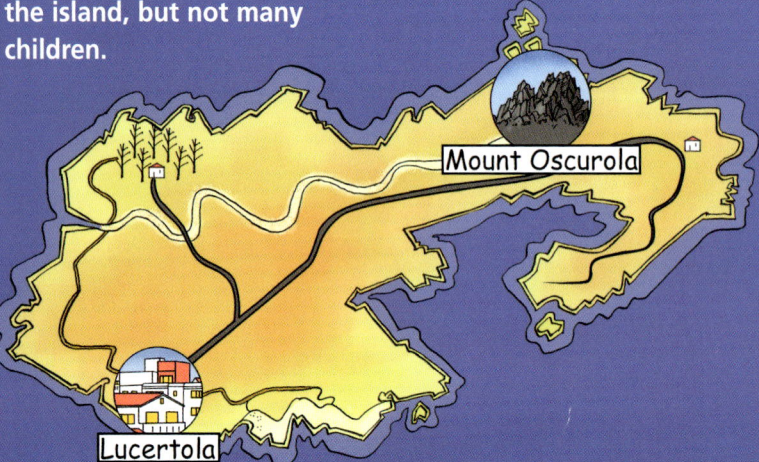

Mount Oscurola

Lucertola

JEFF
Jeff also goes to Lucertola High School. He's in Kaori's class.

SIM-PAT
Sim-Pat is a lizard, but he can talk!

Hi!

TEACHER
Kaori's teacher is very clever. She knows lots of things.

THE LIZARD KING
Who or what is he? No-one knows.

Kaori and the Lizard King

It's Monday morning on the island of Lucertola and Kaori is at school.

LUCERTOLA HIGH SCHOOL

Today Kaori is learning about her country.

DO YOU REMEMBER THE NAME OF THE MOUNTAIN ON OUR ISLAND?

KAORI?

But Kaori isn't listening. She's thinking about Jeff, a boy in her class.

KAORI!

I LOVE YOU, JEFF. I LOVE YOUR EYES, YOUR HAIR... DO YOU LOVE ME, JEFF?

WHAT? UM... I DON'T REMEMBER.
JEFF, DO YOU?
YES, I DO.
THE NAME OF THE MOUNTAIN IS MOUNT OSCUROLA.
VERY GOOD, JEFF.
THANK YOU.
KAORI, SEE ME AFTER THE CLASS!
OH NOOO...

After the class Kaori sees the teacher.

LISTEN TO ME, KAORI. YOU CAN'T LOVE JEFF.

WHY CAN'T I LOVE HIM?

BECAUSE YOU'RE DIFFERENT.

I DON'T WANT TO BE DIFFERENT.

BUT YOU ARE DIFFERENT. AND YOU CAN'T TELL JEFF. IT'S A SECRET.

I DON'T LIKE SECRETS.

IT'S TIME. ARE YOU READY?

YES.

CAPTAIN KAORI IS READY!

AAAARRGH!
OOOF!
VERY GOOD, KAORI!
BUT REMEMBER: WAIT FOR THE RIGHT TIME BEFORE YOU USE YOUR POWERS.
WHEN IS THE RIGHT TIME?
WHEN I TELL YOU.

On Tuesday Kaori goes to school, but something is wrong.

WHERE'S JEFF?

I DON'T KNOW. MAYBE HE'S LATE.

NO. YOU DON'T UNDERSTAND.

I CAN FEEL IT.

SOMETHING IS WRONG!

KAORI, WHERE ARE YOU GOING?

I'M GOING TO FIND JEFF.

STOP. YOU CAN'T LEAVE.

OH, YES, I CAN. DON'T STOP ME.

WHERE'S JEFF? WHERE DO I START? IN THE TOWN? IN HIS HOUSE? OR... DOWN THIS ROAD!

GULP... I DON'T KNOW THIS ROAD. IT'S VERY LONG!

Four hours later...
JEFF! CAN YOU HEAR ME? WHERE ARE YOU?
LISTEN... I CAN HEAR SOMETHING. WHAT IS IT? IT'S GOING VERY FAST.
ROOAR
ROOAR
OH NO! LOOK AT THAT POOR LIZARD. HE'S RUNNING ONTO THE ROAD. STOP! MR. LIZARD! SOMETHING'S COMING!
WHAT?
OH NO!
LUC88036B

I'M HOT... I'M TIRED... I'M HUNGRY... I FEEL TERRIBLE.
HELLO? I'M HERE! CAN YOU SEE ME?
YOU'RE THAT LIZARD. HOW CAN YOU TALK?
IT'S A LONG STORY. MY NAME IS SIM-PAT. WHY ARE YOU SAD?
I'M LOOKING FOR MY FRIEND JEFF.
I CAN'T FIND HIM. YOU CAN'T HELP ME.

YOU'RE WRONG. I CAN HELP YOU.

I KNOW YOUR FRIEND JEFF.

HOW? WHERE IS HE?

ON THE MOUNTAIN?

NOT **ON** THE MOUNTAIN - **IN** THE MOUNTAIN.

IN MOUNT OSCUROLA? I DON'T UNDERSTAND.

LISTEN TO MY STORY...

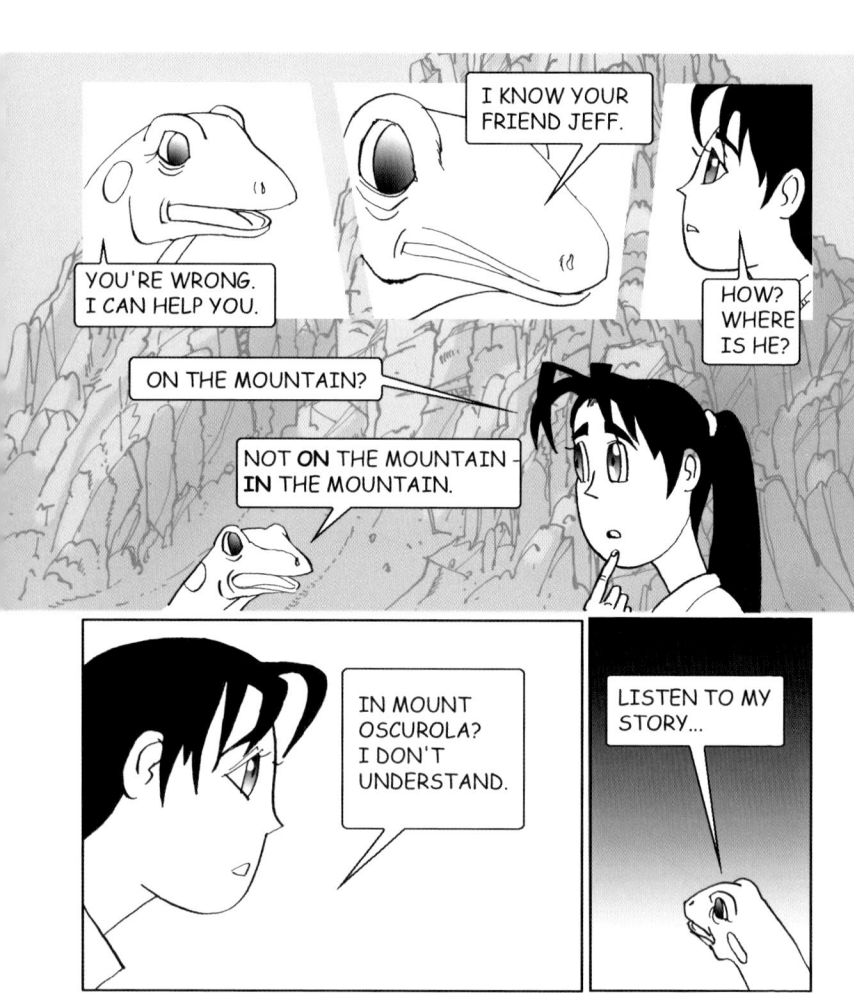

IT'S A DARK NIGHT... A BOY IS CRYING FOR HELP...

HELP!!!

HE'S INSIDE A WATER LORRY. HE'S GOING TO THE MOUNTAIN. HE DOESN'T WANT TO GO.
WHO IS TAKING HIM?
THE BIG LIZARDS! THEY GIVE THE BOY A DRINK...
OPEN YOUR MOUTH!
...AND SLOWLY HE CHANGES INTO A LIZARD.
AAAAAAAAAAAHHHHH!

THE BOY IN THE STORY. HE'S JEFF!

NO. THE BOY IN THE STORY IS SIM-PAT. I'M THAT BOY.

BUT YOU'RE A LIZARD.

NOW I'M A LIZARD.

POOR JEFF! HELP ME FIND HIM BEFORE HE CHANGES TOO!

It's night and Kaori and Sim-Pat climb the mountain.

COME ON!

I'M COMING!

HERE IT IS. COME ON!
DANGER!
IT'S DARK IN HERE.
THERE HE IS!
JEFF! ARE YOU OK?
KAORI! I'M HAPPY TO SEE YOU. HELP ME. I CAN'T OPEN THE DOOR.
I CAN'T OPEN IT! WHAT CAN I DO?
KAORI, CAN YOU HEAR ME?
YES, TEACHER. I CAN HEAR YOU.
THE TIME IS RIGHT. DO YOU UNDERSTAND?
I UNDERSTAND.

JEFF. I HAVE A SECRET TO TELL YOU.
WOW!
NOW I CAN OPEN THE DOOR!
KAORI, YOU'RE GREAT! HOW DO YOU DO THAT?
HUH? WHAT'S HAPPENING TO ME?

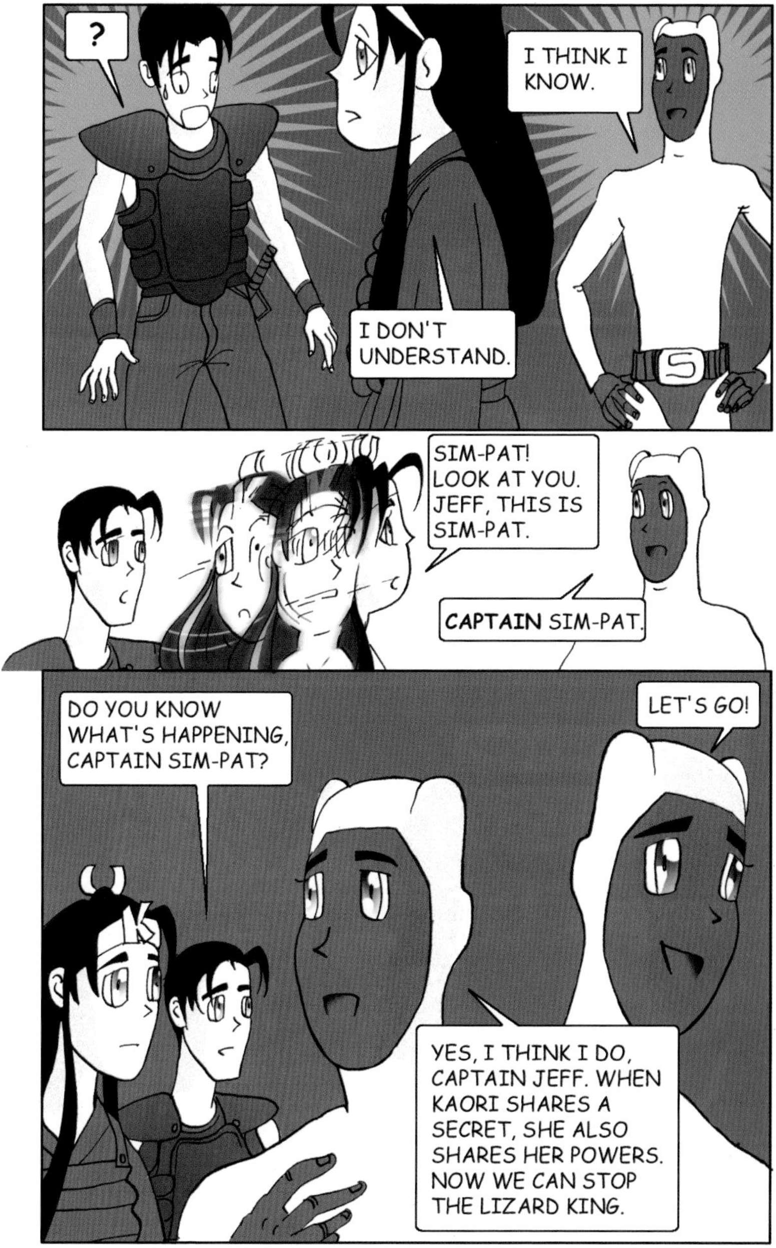
?
I THINK I KNOW.
I DON'T UNDERSTAND.
SIM-PAT! LOOK AT YOU. JEFF, THIS IS SIM-PAT.
CAPTAIN SIM-PAT.
DO YOU KNOW WHAT'S HAPPENING, CAPTAIN SIM-PAT?
YES, I THINK I DO, CAPTAIN JEFF. WHEN KAORI SHARES A SECRET, SHE ALSO SHARES HER POWERS. NOW WE CAN STOP THE LIZARD KING.
LET'S GO!

NOW WHAT DO WE DO?

THERE HE IS, THE LIZARD KING.

LOOK! HE HAS THE ISLAND'S WATER!

HOW MANY CHILDREN THIS MONTH?

FIVE!! THAT'S GOOD.

FIVE, YOUR MAJESTY*.

NAME	SEX	AGE	DATE OF
TINA	F	12	14.09.
MAX	M	8	16.09.
YUKIO	M	16	16.09.
TOKIKO	F	13	17.10.
HASSAN	M	13	19.10.0
MARY	F	10	21.10.0

salamander

AND HOW MUCH WATER?

200 000 LITRES, YOUR MAJESTY.

THAT'S VERY GOOD. I HAVE THE ISLAND'S WATER. I HAVE ITS CHILDREN. NOW LUCERTOLA IS MINE!

*Your majesty: *you say this to a king*

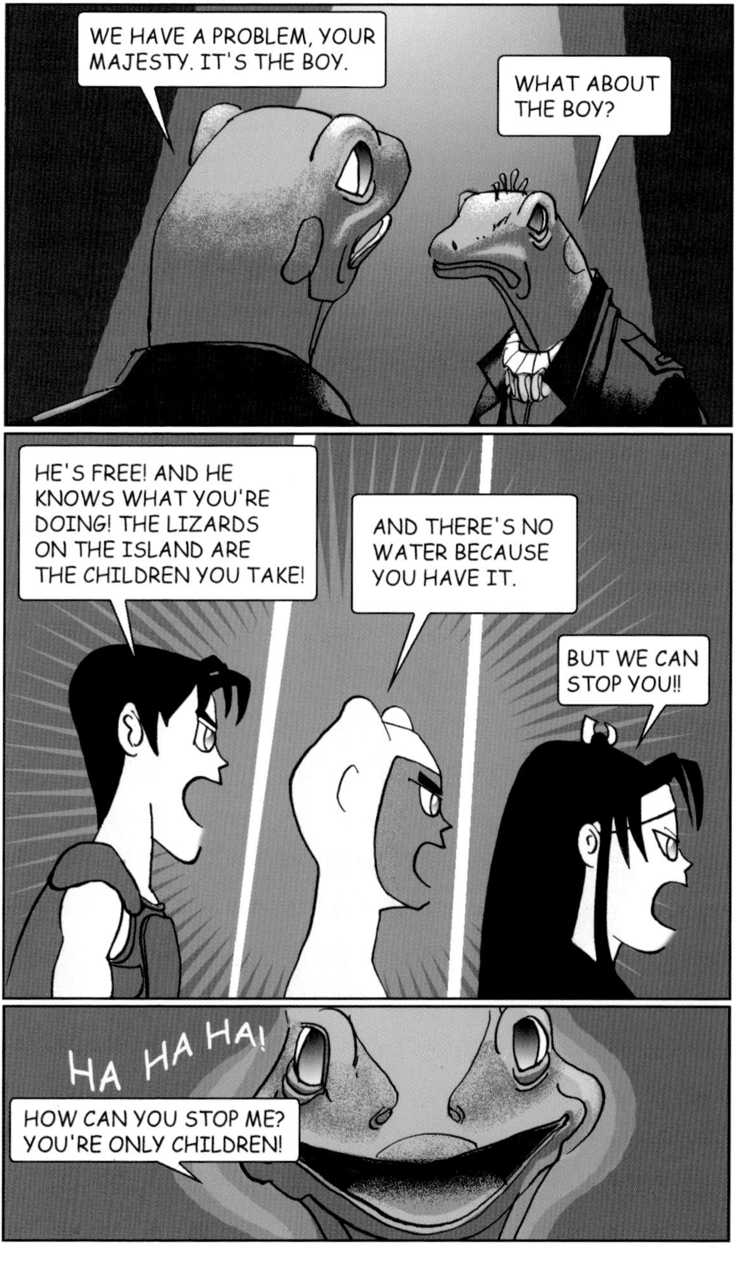
WE HAVE A PROBLEM, YOUR MAJESTY. IT'S THE BOY.
WHAT ABOUT THE BOY?
HE'S FREE! AND HE KNOWS WHAT YOU'RE DOING! THE LIZARDS ON THE ISLAND ARE THE CHILDREN YOU TAKE!
AND THERE'S NO WATER BECAUSE YOU HAVE IT.
BUT WE CAN STOP YOU!!
HA HA HA HA!
HOW CAN YOU STOP ME? YOU'RE ONLY CHILDREN!

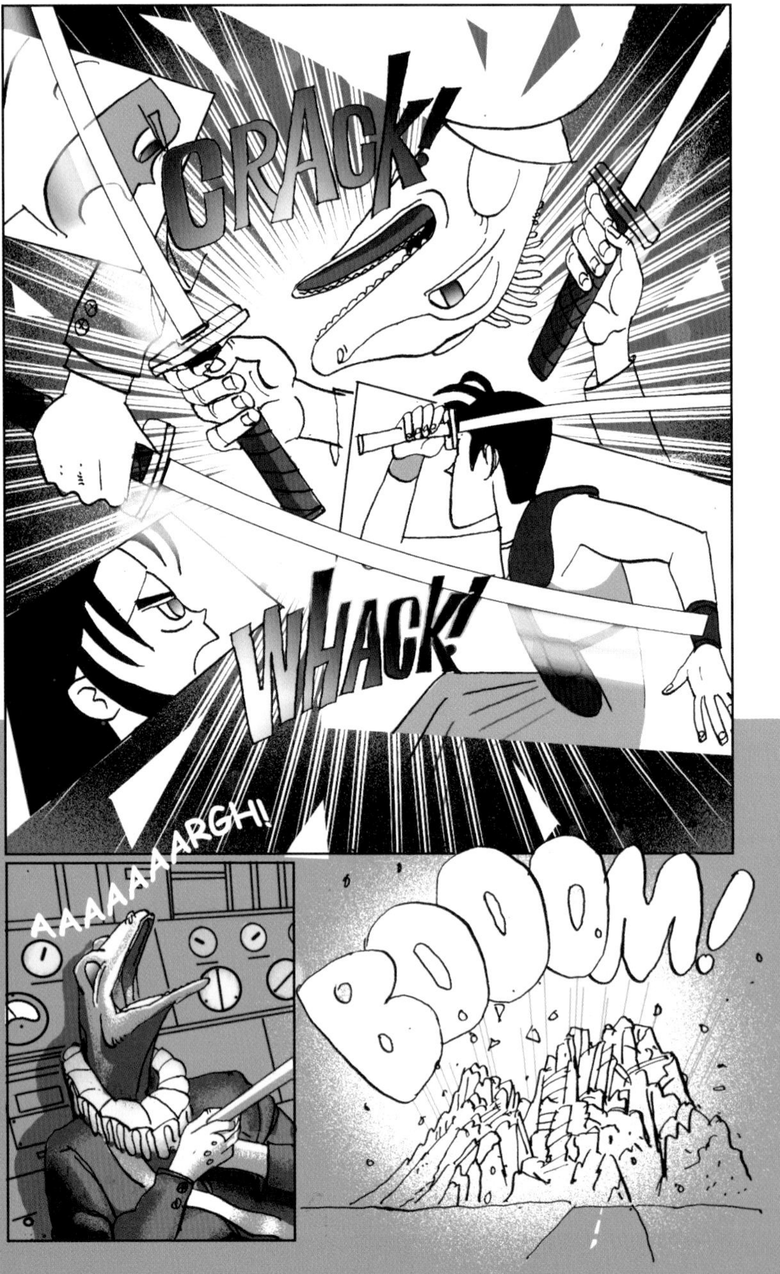
CRACK!
WHACK!
AAAAAAARGH!
BOOOM!

LOOK! IT'S RAINING AGAIN!
AND THE LIZARDS ARE CHANGING INTO CHILDREN AGAIN!
WE HAVE WATER TO DRINK!
THE LIZARD KING AND THE BIG LIZARDS CAN'T DO ANYTHING BAD NOW!
AND LUCERTOLA IS BEAUTIFUL AGAIN!

It's Monday morning on the island of Lucertola and Kaori, Jeff and Sim-Pat are at school.

LUCERTOLA HIGHSCHOOL

Today they are learning about their country.

DO YOU REMEMBER THE NAME OF THE RIVER ON OUR ISLAND, JEFF?

But Jeff isn't listening. He's thinking about Kaori.

I LOVE YOU KAORI. I LOVE YOUR EYES, YOUR HAIR... DO YOU LOVE ME, KAORI?

JEFF, KAORI, SIM-PAT. SEE ME AFTER CLASS.

OH NO!

OH NO!

After class, Kaori, Jeff and Sim-Pat see the teacher.
NO MORE SCHOOL TODAY. YOU HAVE A JOB TO DO. ARE YOU READY?
CAPTAIN SIM-PAT IS READY!
CAPTAIN KAORI IS READY!
CAPTAIN JEFF IS READY!
READY FOR A NEW ADVENTURE! LET'S GO!
WHOOSH!

FACT FILE

MANGA

Kaori and the Lizard King **is like a manga comic book. What is manga? Here are ten facts about manga.**

1 Manga comes from Japan.

2 In Japanese manga means "comic book".

3 Girls and boys in many countries love these comics.

4 Manga comics are more than 65 years old. The idea comes from 200-year-old Japanese pictures.

What do these words mean? You can look in a dictionary.
comic   hero/heroes   film

FACTS

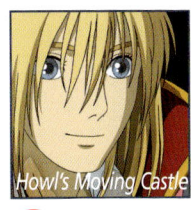

5 You read Japanese manga books from right to left and not left to right.

6 There are different manga comics for boys and girls. *Shonen* manga is for boys and *Shojo* manga is for girls.

Howl's Moving Castle

7 Stories in manga comics can be two or three years long!

8 One famous manga by Osamu Tezuka has 3,000 pages.

9 The heroes of manga stories are usually teenagers. They have special powers but they don't always know this.

10 The name for manga films like *Spirited Away*, is *anime*.

Spirited Away

Make a Manga

Do you like manga? Look at the picture of Kaori. Can you draw her picture?
Take a pencil and some paper. Look at her head. Now look at her hair, her eyes, nose and mouth.
Is your picture good?
Now draw a manga picture of a friend!

27

FACT FILE
FANTASY

Lucertola is not a real place. It's a fantasy world. There are many famous fantasy worlds. Read about these fantasy worlds and answer these questions:

1. Where do children never grow old?
2. Where can animals talk?
3. Who grows tall and then grows small?
4. Who has a ring?

Narnia

The Lion, the Witch and the Wardrobe is one of seven fantasy stories in *The Chronicles of Narnia* by C. S. Lewis. In the fantasy world of Narnia, animals can talk and there is lots of magic.

The Lion, the Witch and the Wardrobe is now a film. In the story, four children find a door to Narnia inside a wardrobe. They find a new world. It's always winter there. They meet Aslan the lion. He helps them and they fight the White Witch. Winter ends.

What do these words mean? You can look in a dictionary.

fantasy   fight   magic   winter   world

Main picture: *The Lion, the Witch and the Wardrobe*, 2005

WORLDS

Neverland

Neverland is the fantasy island in J. M. Barrie's story of *Peter Pan*. In the story, Wendy and her brothers go with Peter to Neverland. In Neverland, children never grow old.

The children live on the island with the Lost Boys, Indians, Captain Hook, and his pirates. In the film *Finding Neverland*, Johnny Depp is J.M. Barrie, the writer.

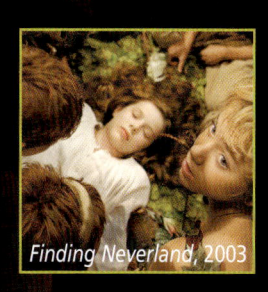

Finding Neverland, 2003

Middle-Earth

Middle-Earth is the fantasy world of *The Lord of the Rings* by J. R. R. Tolkien. It is Britain's favourite book – and it's very long!

The story of *The Lord of the Rings* starts with a birthday party for Frodo Baggins. Frodo is a Hobbit. Hobbits are not the same as people. They are smaller. In the story, Frodo has a magic Ring. He wears the Ring and people can't see him. The actor Elijah Wood is Frodo in the film.

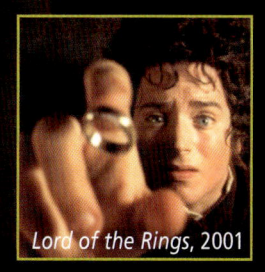

Lord of the Rings, 2001

Wonderland

In *Alice's Adventures in Wonderland* by Lewis Carroll, a girl follows a rabbit into a fantasy world. In Wonderland, Alice grows tall and then grows small. She meets a baby. It changes into a pig and a cat. And she drinks tea at a party that never ends. Wonderland is a magic place where animals can talk. At the end of the story Alice goes back to the real world.

Alice in Wonderland, 1972

Can you find these words in the pictures?
grow small   ring   wardrobe

SELF-STUDY ACTIVITIES

Pages 1–5: At School

Before you read

1 Make parts of the body with the letters.
   - **a)** seey
   - **b)** rahi
   - **c)** homut
   - **d)** seno
   - **e)** teef

2 Match these words to make useful phrases.
   - **a)** Very — to me.
   - **b)** Thank — ready?
   - **c)** Do you — good.
   - **d)** Listen — remember?
   - **e)** Are you — you.

3 Match the questions with the answers.
   - **a)** What are you listening to?
   - **b)** Are you happy?
   - **c)** Who are you thinking about?
   - **d)** What are you learning at school?
   - **e)** Do you remember the answer?
   - **i)** Yes, I do.
   - **ii)** My brother.
   - **iii)** The radio.
   - **iv)** Yes, I am.
   - **v)** English.

After you read

4 True or false?
   - **a)** Lucertola is an island.
   - **b)** It's Saturday morning.
   - **c)** Jeff is a teacher.
   - **d)** Mount Oscurola is a mountain.
   - **e)** Kaori has a secret.

5 Put these sentences in the correct order.
   - **a)** Kaori: I don't want to be different.
   - **b)** Teacher: It's time. Are you ready?
   - **c)** Kaori: Why can't I love him?
   - **d)** Teacher: But you are different. And you can't tell Jeff. It's a secret.
   - **e)** Kaori: Yes.
   - **f)** Teacher: Listen to me, Kaori. You can't love Jeff.
   - **g)** Kaori: I don't like secrets.
   - **h)** Teacher: Because you're different.

Pages 6–11: On the Road

Before you read

6 Complete the sentences using one of the words.

hungry   sad   hot   tired

   a) I'm _____. I want to sleep.
   b) Can we eat? I'm very _____.
   c) I'm _____ because the holidays are ending.
   d) It's a sunny day and I'm _____.

7 Match the two halves of the sentences.

   a) The car   i) is running onto the road.
   b) The small boy   ii) my friend.
   c) I'm looking for   iii) next to the teacher.
   d) They're sitting   iv) is going very fast.

After you read

8 Choose the correct preposition.

in   down   in   into   onto

   a) Kaori walks _____ the road.
   b) Sim Pat runs _____ the road.
   c) Sim Pat says Jeff is _____ the mountain.
   d) In Sim Pat's story, the boy is _____ the lorry.
   e) The boy changes _____ a lizard.

9 Answer these questions.

   a) What does Kaori hear on the road?
   b) Can Sim Pat help Kaori?
   c) In Sim-Pat's story, where does the boy go?
   d) What do the big lizards give the boy?
   e) What happens when the boy drinks?
   f) Who is the boy in the story?

SELF-STUDY ACTIVITIES

Pages 12–20: In the Mountain

Before you read
10 Which of these nouns is not a person?
   a) mother   b) father   c) lizard
   d) teacher   e) boy   f) girl

11 Put the verbs into the correct sentences.
   a) changing   i) I have a story to _____ you.
   b) has   ii) I can't _____ the window.
   c) is raining   iii) Look! He _____ big feet.
   d) open   iv) It _____ today!
   e) tell   v) I'm _____ my clothes because I'm hot.

After you read
12 What do these comic words describe?
   a) HA HA HA!
   b) CRACK! WHACK!
   c) AAAAAAARGH!
   d) WHOOSH!

   i) Kaori, Jeff and Sim-Pat flying off for a new adventure.
   ii) Kaori, Jeff and Sim-Pat hitting the Lizard King.
   iii) The Lizard King laughing.
   iv) The Lizard King feeling angry.

13 What do you think?
   a) Is it good to share secrets?
   b) Which is your favourite character?
   c) What do you think happens in Kaori's new adventure?